SandCastle™

Baby African Animals

It's a Baby Rhinoceros!

Kelly Doudna

Consulting Editor, Diane Craig, M.A./Reading Specialist

ABDO
Publishing Company

Published by ABDO Publishing Company, 8000 West 78th Street, Edina, Minnesota 55439.

Copyright © 2009 by Abdo Consulting Group, Inc. International copyrights reserved in all countries.

No part of this book may be reproduced in any form without written permission from the publisher. SandCastle™ is a trademark and logo of ABDO Publishing Company.

Printed in the United States.

Editor: Liz Salzmann
Content Developer: Nancy Tuminelly
Cover and Interior Design and Production: Mighty Media
Photo Credits: iStockPhoto (Henri Faure, Cliff Parnell, Michael Price, Vova Pomortzeff), Peter Arnold Inc. (Martin Harvey, BIOS Klein, Gerard Lacz, A. Rouse), ShutterStock

Library of Congress Cataloging-in-Publication Data

Doudna, Kelly, 1963-
  It's a baby rhinoceros! / Kelly Doudna.
    p. cm. -- (Baby African animals)
  ISBN 978-1-60453-158-9
  1. Rhinoceroses--Infancy--Juvenile literature. I. Title.

QL737.U63D68 2009
599.66'8139--dc22
                              2008014115

SandCastle™ Level: Transitional

SandCastle™ books are created by a team of professional educators, reading specialists, and content developers around five essential components—phonemic awareness, phonics, vocabulary, text comprehension, and fluency—to assist young readers as they develop reading skills and strategies and increase their general knowledge. All books are written, reviewed, and leveled for guided reading, early reading intervention, and Accelerated Reader® programs for use in shared, guided, and independent reading and writing activities to support a balanced approach to literacy instruction. The SandCastle™ series has four levels that correspond to early literacy development. The levels are provided to help teachers and parents select appropriate books for young readers.

Emerging Readers	**Beginning Readers**	**Transitional Readers**	**Fluent Readers**
(no flags)	(1 flag)	(2 flags)	(3 flags)

SandCastle™ would like to hear from you. Please send us your comments and suggestions.
sandcastle@abdopublishing.com

Vital Statistics

for the Rhinoceros

BABY NAME
calf

NUMBER IN LITTER
1

WEIGHT AT BIRTH
80 to 140 pounds

AGE OF INDEPENDENCE
2 to 3 years

ADULT WEIGHT
1,760 to 7,920 pounds

LIFE EXPECTANCY
40 years

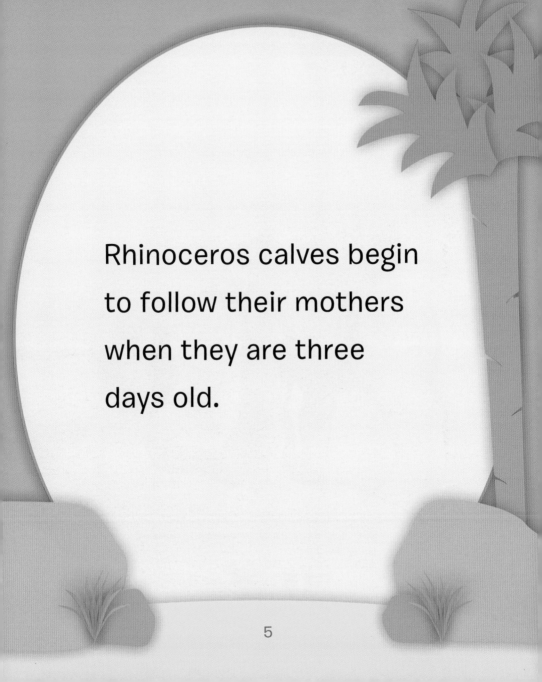

Rhinoceros calves begin to follow their mothers when they are three days old.

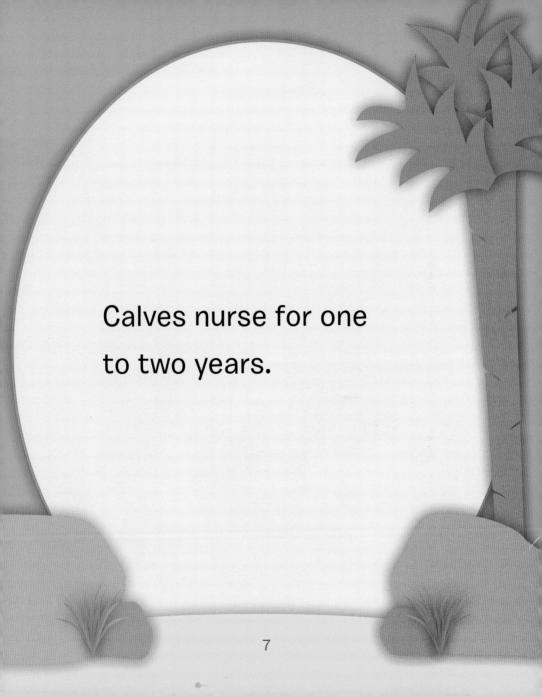

Calves nurse for one to two years.

Some rhinos have square lips. They eat grass. Other rhinos have pointed lips. They eat leaves and twigs.

All rhinoceroses are herbivores.

Rhinoceroses make many different sounds. They grunt, snort, bellow, and squeak.

Hyenas and lions prey on
rhinoceros calves.

Mother rhinos are
very protective of
their calves.

Rhinos have excellent senses of hearing and smell. But they have very poor eyesight.

A rhinoceros might attack a tree or a rock if it feels threatened.

Rhinoceroses wallow
in the mud to stay cool.
The coating of mud
helps protect them
from parasites.

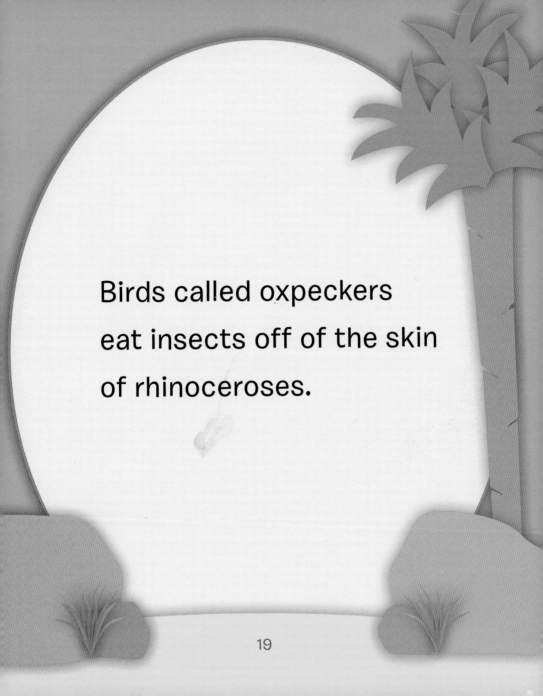

Birds called oxpeckers
eat insects off of the skin
of rhinoceroses.

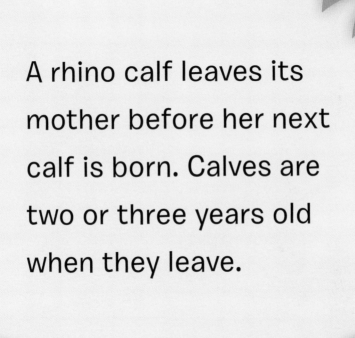

A rhino calf leaves its mother before her next calf is born. Calves are two or three years old when they leave.

Fun Fact
About the Rhinoceros

The horn of a rhinoceros can grow to be as long as five feet. That's longer than most 5th graders are tall!

Glossary

birth – the moment when a person or animal is born.

expectancy – an expected or likely amount.

herbivore – an animal that eats mainly plants.

independence – no longer needing others to care for or support you.

insect – a small creature with two or four wings, six legs, and a body with three sections.

nurse – to feed a baby milk from the breast.

parasite – an organism that lives and feeds on or in a different organism without contributing to the host's survival.

prey – to hunt or catch an animal for food.

protect – to guard someone or something from harm or danger.

threatened – frightened by something.

twig – a thin, small branch of a tree or a bush.

wallow – to roll around in water, snow, or mud.

To see a complete list of SandCastle™ books and other nonfiction titles from ABDO Publishing Company, visit **www.abdopublishing.com**.
8000 West 78th Street, Edina, MN 55439
800-800-1312 • 952-831-1632 fax